T0039840

Page 15
Page 17
Page 19
Page 21
Thumbelina
The Three Bears
Cinderella
Little Red Riding Hood
Page 23

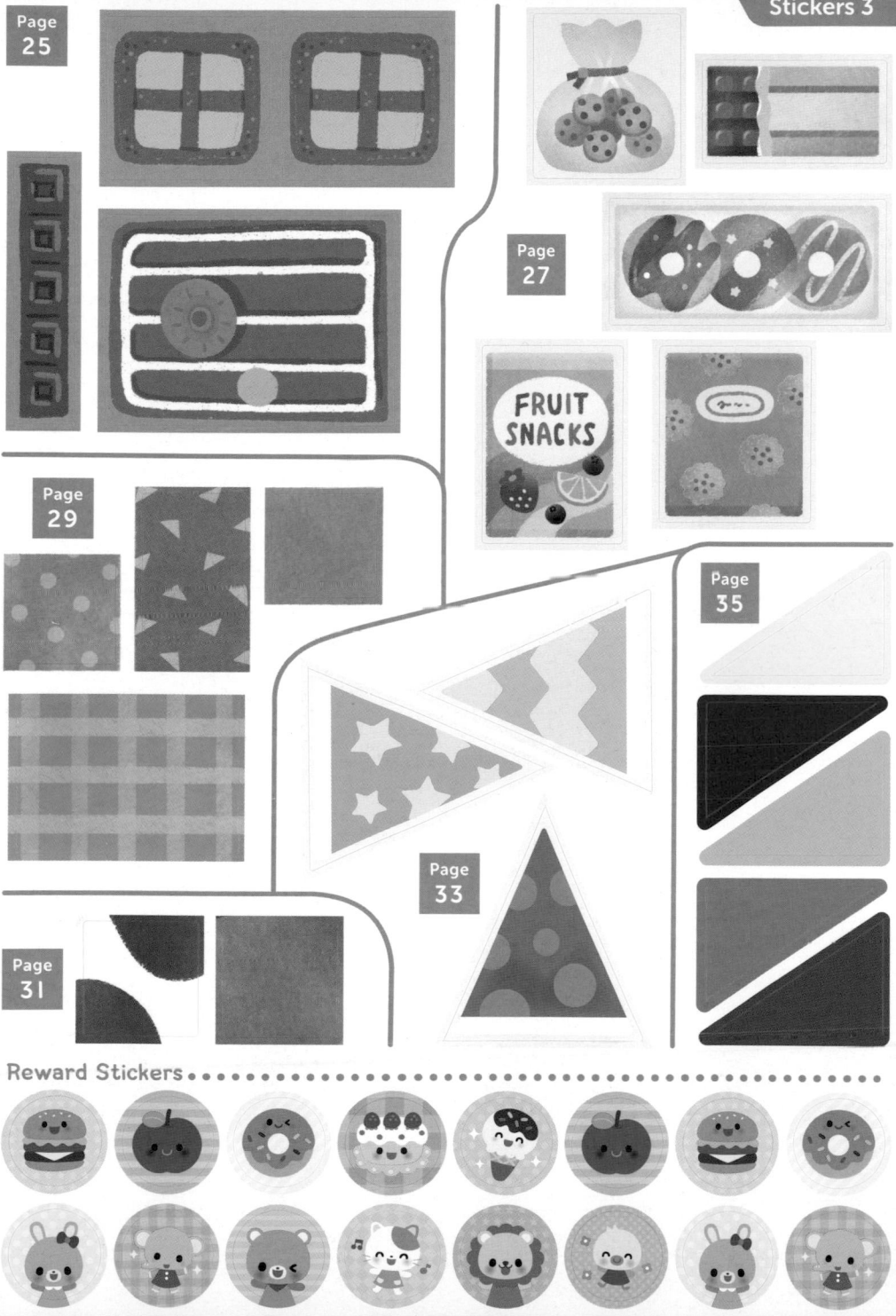
Page 25
Page 27
FRUIT SNACKS
Page 29
Page 35
Page 33
Page 31
Reward Stickers

Page 37
Page 39
Page 41
Page 43
Page 45
Reward Stickers

Page 47
Page 49
FARM
Page 51
Page 53
Reward Stickers

Page 55
Page 57
Page 59
Page 61
POLICE

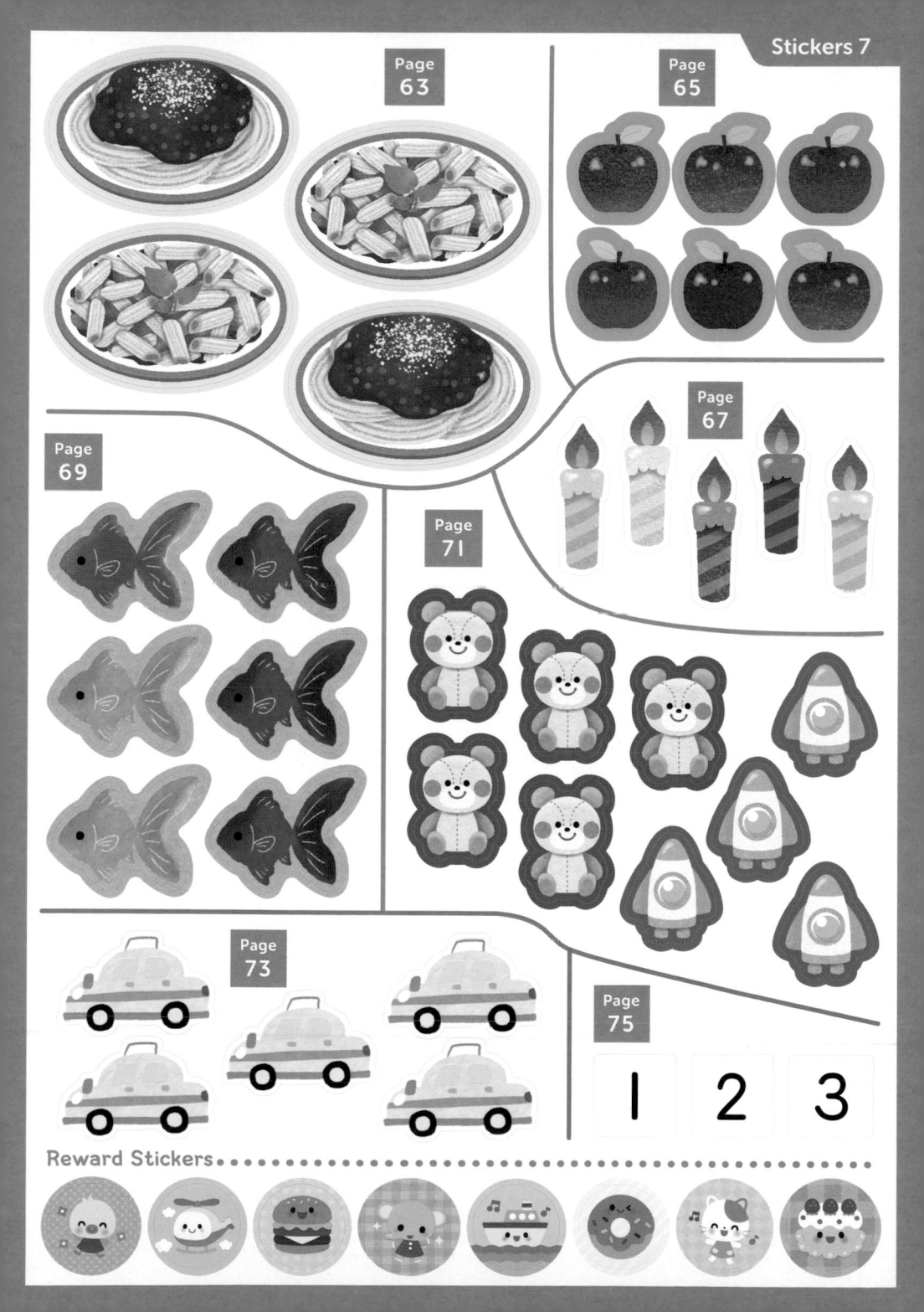
Page 63
Page 65
Page 67
Page 69
Page 71
Page 73
Page 75
1
2
3
Reward Stickers

Page 77

1 2 3 4 5

Page 81

6 7 8 9 10

Page 79

Page 83

Page 85

1 2 3

Page 87

1 2 2 3 4 5 5 6

7 8 9 10

Page 89

1

2

3

Page 91

1

2

3

4

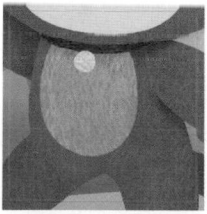

5

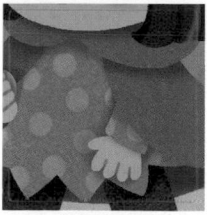

6

Reward Stickers

Note to Parents

1) The activities in this book are at an appropriate developmental level so your child can do them independently. But don't hesitate to help them! When parents are involved in the learning process, it increases a child's intellectual curiosity and creates a more effective, supportive learning environment.

2) To support your child's learning, review the **"To Parents"** section featured below the instructions. These tips offer effective ways to explain the activity to your child.

3) Desides the **sticker activities**, this book includes **additional activities** that use pencils and crayons to develop school readiness skills. By alternating between the sticker pages and the other activities, children will learn to classify by color, shape, and size while boosting observation, self-confidence, self-esteem, vocabulary, creativity, and problem-solving skills.

4) When your child finishes the additional activities, let them choose a **reward sticker** to put on the page. Be sure to also praise your child's good work! Be specific with your praise, saying something like, "You did a good job counting!" or "You were very patient!"

Counting 1 to 10

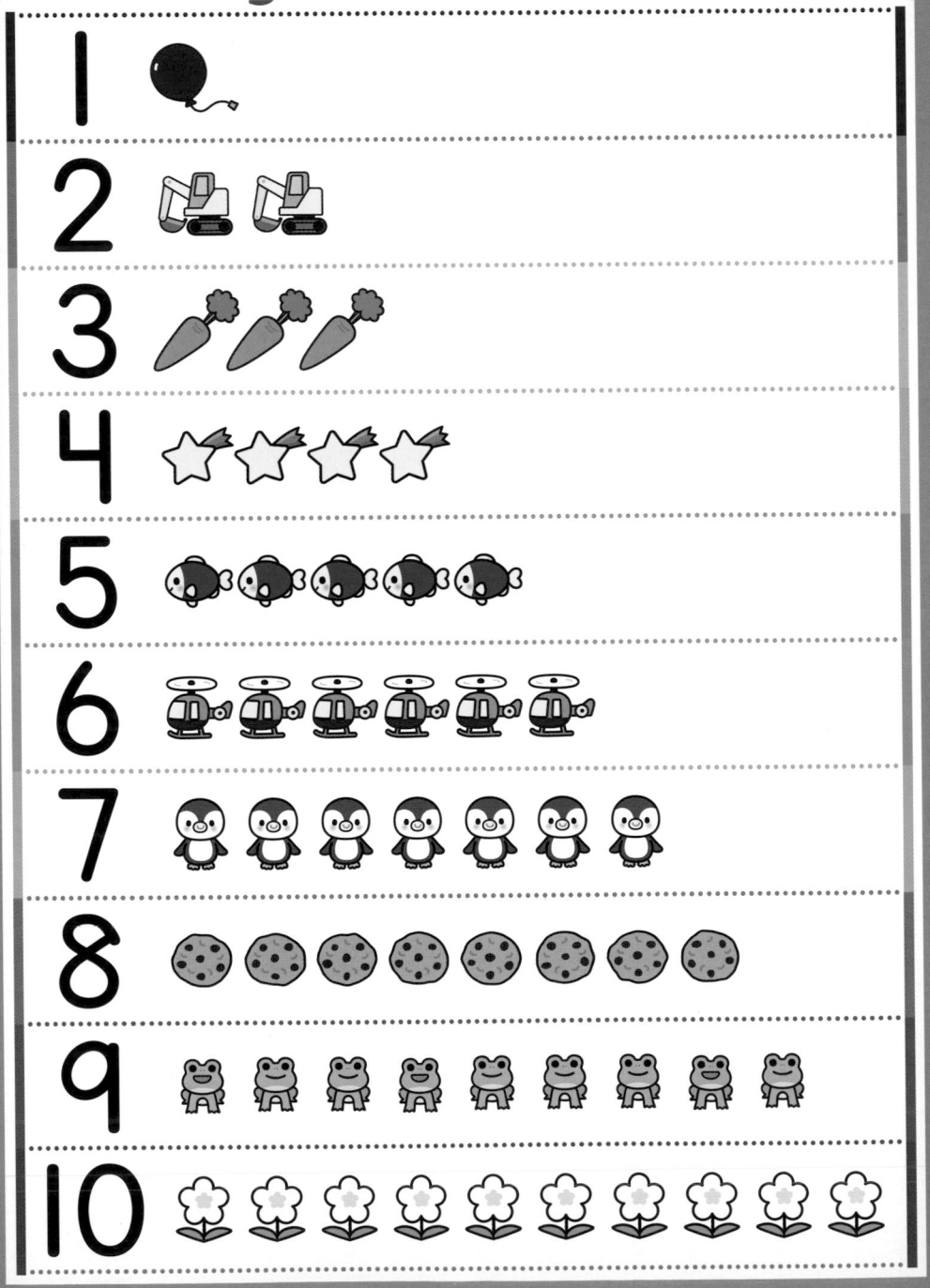

Level 1 ★☆☆

Yellow Chicks

Put yellow chick stickers on the grass.

To Parents Encourage your child to put stickers on the free space so they do not overlap the pictures of the chicken or chick.

Level 1 ★☆☆

Name the Color

Good job!

Say the color of each stuffed animal.

To Parents Once your child can say each color, have them say both the color and name of the toy, such as red bear and yellow bunny.

Busy Cars

Put red car stickers on the road.

Find the Blue Animals

Level 1 ★☆☆

Good job!

Find the blue sea animals and point to them.

Fresh Vegetables

Find and add stickers to complete each vegetable.

To Parents When your child is finished, say the color and name of each vegetable, such as red tomato, purple eggplant, and yellow corn.

Yummy Ice Cream Cones

Level 1 ★☆☆

Good job!

Find the ice cream cone that matches the one in the box and point to it.

To Parents First ask your child to name the color of each ice cream cone, then find one that matches the example.

Level 1 ★☆☆

Cheerful Flowers

Put blue flower stickers on the tables.

To Parents This activity allows your child to practice applying stickers to a limited space.

Level 1 ★☆☆

Color Match

Good job!

Draw a line from ● to ● to match the color in each circle to the color of each animal.

To Parents Once your child can connect the lines, say both the color and animal, such as white bear and gray elephant.

Level 1 ★☆☆

Summer Fun

Put circle stickers on their matching shadows.

To Parents Encourage your child to find the large and small circles before adding the stickers.

Level 1 ★☆☆

Color Match

Draw lines from ★ to ●.

Good job!

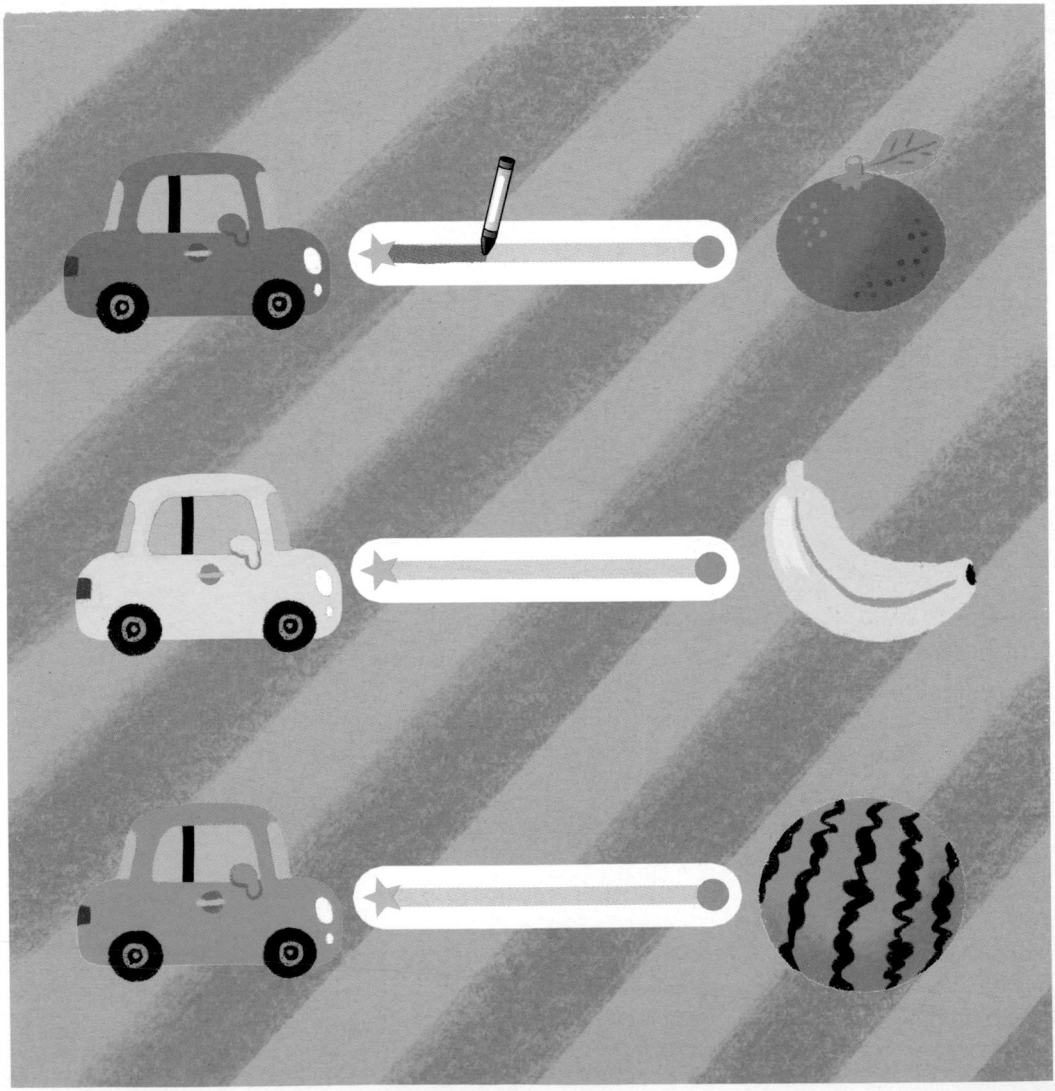

Level 1 ★☆☆

Around and Around

Put circle stickers on their matching shadows.

To Parents All circles are the same size. It is okay if your child adds the stickers and they are not aligned with the shadows. They will gradually be able to achieve this.

Level 1 ★☆☆

Vegetable Stand

Good job!

Find the green vegetables and point to them.

Level 1 ★☆☆

Freshly Baked Bread

Put circle stickers on their matching shadows.

Level 2 ★★☆

Clothes Match

Good job!

Find the outfit that matches the one in the box and point to it.

Level 2 ★★☆

Beautiful Butterfly

Put circle stickers on their matching shadows to complete the butterfly.

To Parents The circle stickers are now a little smaller. Tell your child to make a beautiful butterfly and encourage them to put stickers wherever they like.

Find the Same Giraffe

Level 2 ★★☆

Good job!

Find the giraffe that matches the one in the box and point to it.

To Parents Encourage your child to pay attention to the giraffe's pattern and color. Ask them to point to the yellow giraffes, then have them notice the different patterns on their bodies.

Level 2 ★★☆

Cheerful Pattern

Put circle stickers on their matching shadows to finish the pattern.

Level 1 ★☆☆

Draw Curved Lines

Good job!

Draw lines from ★ to ●.

Level 1 ★☆☆

Favorite Stories

Put rectangle stickers on their matching shadows.

To Parents Encourage your child to put stickers on the gray squares. If this is difficult, help them by placing one corner of the sticker down first and adjust from there.

Level 1 ★☆☆

Name the Shape

Good job!

Trace each shape with your finger.
Then, say the shape's name.

circle

rectangle

square

diamond

triangle

star

Level 1 ★☆☆

Colorful Trains

Put rectangle stickers on their matching shadows.

To Parents Use the train's colors and patterns to identify the matching train car stickers.

Level 1 ★☆☆

Toy Store

Find the circle-shaped toys and point to them.

Good job!

Level 2 ★★☆

Candy Cottage

Put square and rectangle stickers on their matching shadows.

Level 2 ★★☆

Draw a Circle

Draw a line from ★ to ●.

Good job!

To Parents If your child has difficulty tracing, put your hand on theirs to help them draw.

Level 2 ★★☆

Sweet Treats

Put rectangle stickers on their matching shadows.

Level 1 ★☆☆

Party Time

Good job!

Find the square-shaped presents and point to them.

Level 2 ★★☆

Rainbow Castle

Put square and rectangle stickers on their matching shadows.

Through to the Park

Draw a line from ➡ to ➡.

Level 1 ★☆☆

Good job!

To Parents Encourage your child to stop drawing when they need to change direction, then start again.

Level 1 ★☆☆

Colors and Patterns

Find and add stickers to complete each animal.

To Parents Make sure to put the cow pattern sticker in the right direction.

Level 1 ★☆☆

Treasure Chests

Good job!

Draw a line from ➡ to ➡ through each rectangular treasure chest.

To Parents If your child has difficulty drawing long lines, encourage them to take a break when they reach each treasure chest and then start again.

Level 1 ★☆☆

Happy Birthday

Put triangle stickers on their matching shadows.

To Parents It might be difficult for your child to place triangle-shaped stickers. Put one corner down first and adjust it from there.

Level 1 ★☆☆

My Neighborhood

Good job!

Find the houses with a triangle-shaped roof and point to them.

Level 2 ★★☆

Cruising Sailboats

Put triangle stickers on their matching shadows.

Level 1 ★☆☆

Happy Hats

Good job!

Find the triangle-shaped hats and point to them.

Level 2 ★★☆

Pizza Party

Put triangle stickers on their matching shadows.

To Parents Make sure each pizza slice is pointing in the right direction.

Spot the Differences

Level 1 ★☆☆

Good job!

Find two differences between the top and bottom picture.

To Parents The star on the boy's shirt and the triangle block are different in these pictures.

Level 2 ★★☆

My Community

Put triangle stickers on their matching shadows.

Level 1 ★☆☆

Connect the Dots

Connect the dots in order: 1 → 2 → 3 → 1.

Good job!

Level 3 ★★★

Fruit Snacks

Put fruit stickers on their matching shadows.

To Parents Guide your child to match the stickers in order from easiest to hardest: melon, orange, watermelon, apple.

Spot the Differences

Level 2 ★★☆

Good job!

Find three differences between the top and bottom picture.

To Parents The squirrel, bird, and cat's food are different in these pictures.

Level 3 ★★★

Animals in the Zoo

Put animal stickers on their matching shadows.

To Parents Ask your child to identify the animal shadows. Have them pay attention to animal features such as the elephant's trunk, the panda's ears, and the lion's mane.

Level 1 ★☆☆

Lunchtime

Good job!

Find the food that matches the one in the box and point to it.

Level 3 ★★★

Swimming Sea Animals

Put sea animal stickers on their matching shadows.

Level 1 ★☆☆

Animal Match

Good job!

Draw a line from ● to ● to match each animal with its face.

Level 3 ★★★

Petting Zoo

Put animal stickers on their matching shadows.

Level 1 ★☆☆

Frosty Maze

Draw a line from ➡ to ➡.

Good job!

To Parents Start by tracing the path with your finger. Then, draw a line with a pencil or crayon.

Level 3 ★★★

Favorite Toy

Put toy stickers on their matching shadows.

Level 2 ★★☆

Draw a Star

Draw a line from ★ to ●.

Good job!

To Parents Encourage your child to stop at each corner. It is okay if they go outside of the gray line as long as it is within the white border. Praise your child when they trace well!

Level 2 ★★☆

Amusement Park

Put stickers on their matching shadows.

Spot the Differences

Level 2 ★★☆

Good job!

Find two differences between the top and bottom picture.

To Parents The girl's outfit and the boy's pants are different in the pictures.

Level 3 ★★★

Cool Clothes

Put clothing stickers on their matching shadows.

To Parents Put one part of the sticker on first, such as the sleeve, and adjust from there.

Spot the Differences

Level 2 ★★☆

Good job!

Find two differences between the top and bottom picture.

To Parents The lion's mane, the purple balloon, and the merry-go-round are different in the pictures.

Level 3 ★★★

Animal Puzzles

Put stickers on their matching shadows.
Complete the picture so it matches the example.

example

Level 1 ★☆☆

Color the Stars

Color the stars with your favorite color.

Good job!

To Parents Color the star pattern with your child. It is okay if your child colors outside of the stars.

Level 3 ★★★

Up and Away!

Put stickers on their matching shadows.
Complete the picture so it matches the example.

To Parents Align the circle sticker with the mouse's face and the bird's tail.

example

Color the Diamonds

Level 1 ★☆☆

Good job!

Color the diamond shapes with your favorite color.

Level 3 ★★★

Playground Puzzle

Put stickers on their matching shadows.
Complete the picture so it matches the example.

Match the Vehicle Parts

Draw a line from ● to ● to match each vehicle with its part.

Level 2 ★★☆

Good job!

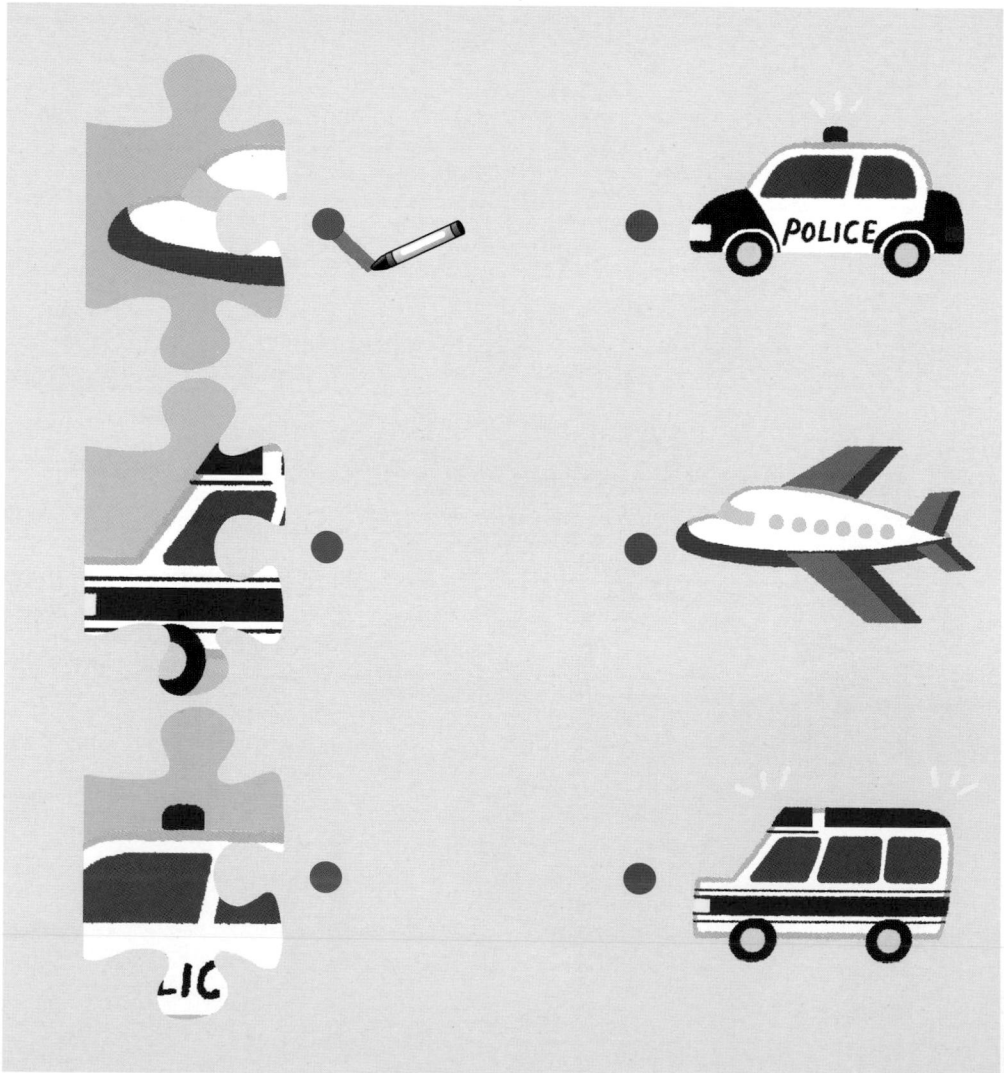

Level 3 ★★★

Busy Vehicles Puzzle

Put stickers on their matching shadows.
Complete the picture so it matches the example.

To Parents Following the example, have your child pay attention to the color and shape of each vehicle.

example

Collect the Puzzle Pieces

Level 1 ★☆☆

Good job!

Draw a line from ➡ to ➡ and collect the puzzle pieces on the path.

Dining Out

Put a sticker on the place mats so each animal has a plate of pasta.

To Parents The number of animals and plates of pasta is the same. This is called one-to-one correspondence. After each animal has a plate of pasta, praise your child by saying, "Good job."

Level 1 ★☆☆

Favorite Things

Good job!

Draw a line from ➡ to ➡ and collect the cat's favorite things on the path.

Level 1 ★☆☆

Apple Orchard

Put two apple stickers on each tree.

Level 1 ★☆☆

Find the Number I

Good job!

Find the number I and trace it with your favorite color.

Level 1 ★☆☆

Birthday Candles

Put candle stickers on each cake to match the age of each child.

Level 1 ★☆☆

Find the Number 2

Good job!

Find the number 2 and trace it with your favorite color.

Level 2 ★★☆

Count the Goldfish

Put goldfish stickers in each tank so it matches the number on the left.

one

1

two

2

three

3

Level 1 ★☆☆

Find the Number 3

Good job!

Find the number 3 and trace it with your favorite color.

Level 2 ★★☆

Count the Toys

Put toy stickers in the blue and red toy boxes so they match the number on the left.

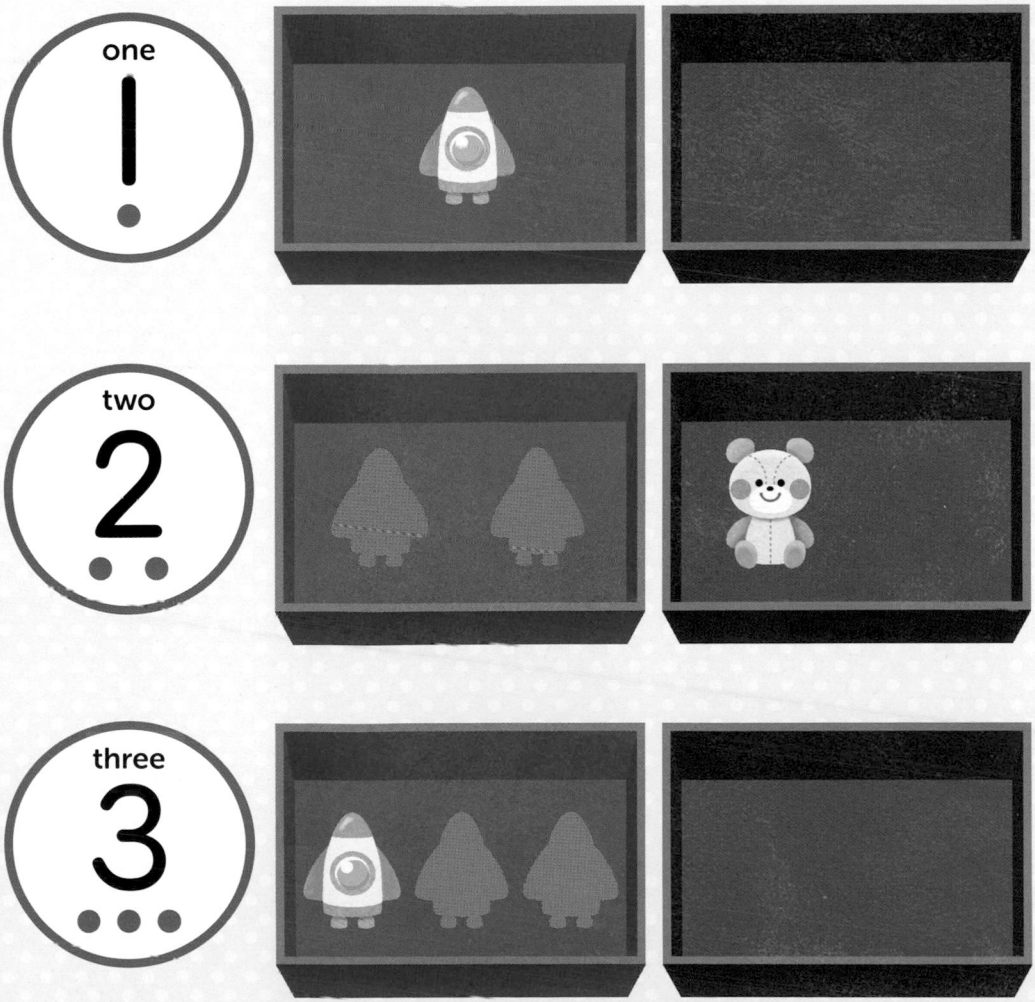

Level 1 ★☆☆

Playful Pets

Good job!

Count the dogs. Then, color the same number of ◯ with your favorite color.

To Parents If this seems difficult, draw circles around the dogs and then draw lines to connect them to the circles below.

Level 1 ★☆☆

Taxis in the City

Count the taxis. Then, put the matching number of taxi stickers in the box below.

Level 2 ★★☆

Count the Sweets

Count the chocolate chip cookies, cherry cookies, and candies. Then, color the same number of ○ as each sweet with your favorite color.

Good job!

To Parents This activity practices identifying and counting objects that are similar shapes. If this seems difficult, color each row of circles with a different color.

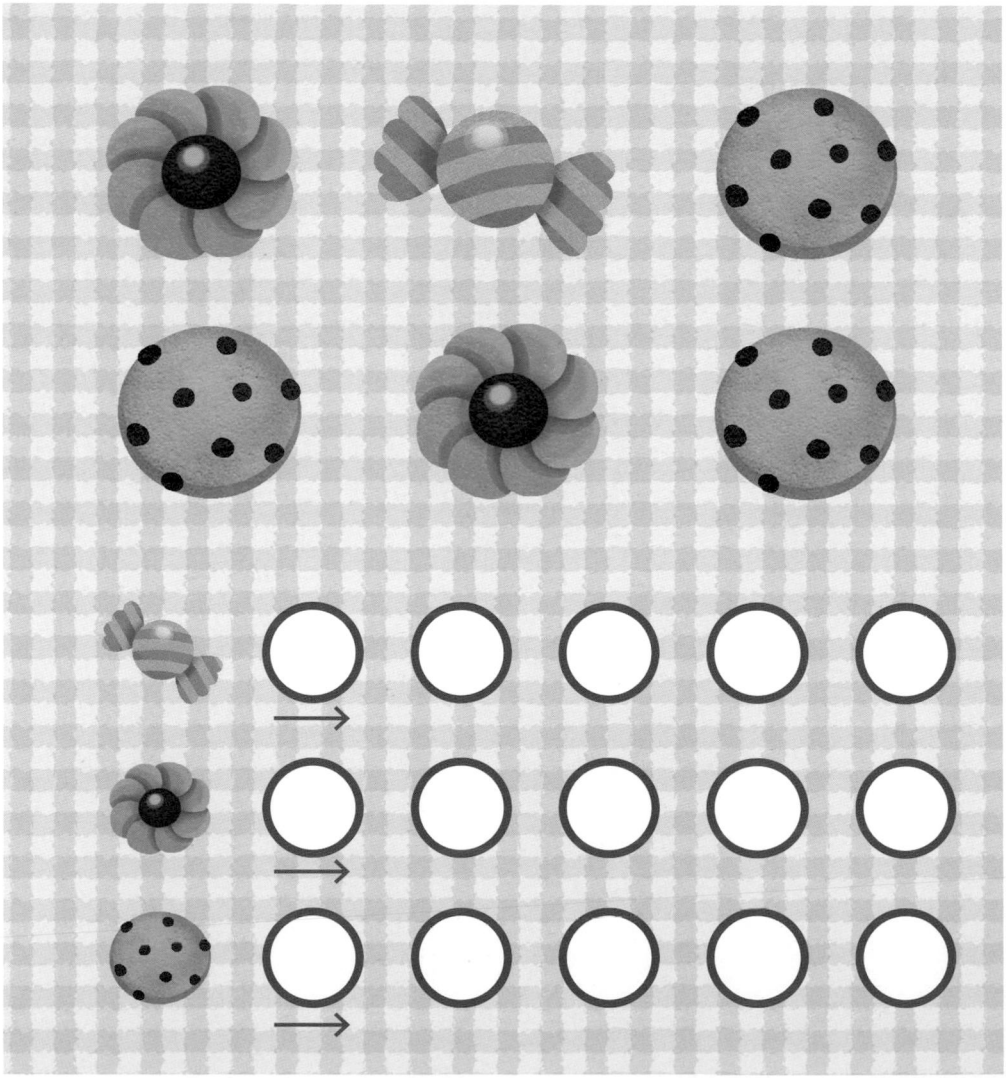

Level 1 ★☆☆

Zoom Zoom!

Count the kids on each ride.
Then, put the matching number sticker on □.

Count the School Supplies

Level 2 ★★☆

Good job!

Count the scissors, crayons, and rolls of tape. Then, color the same number of ○ as each school supply with your favorite color.

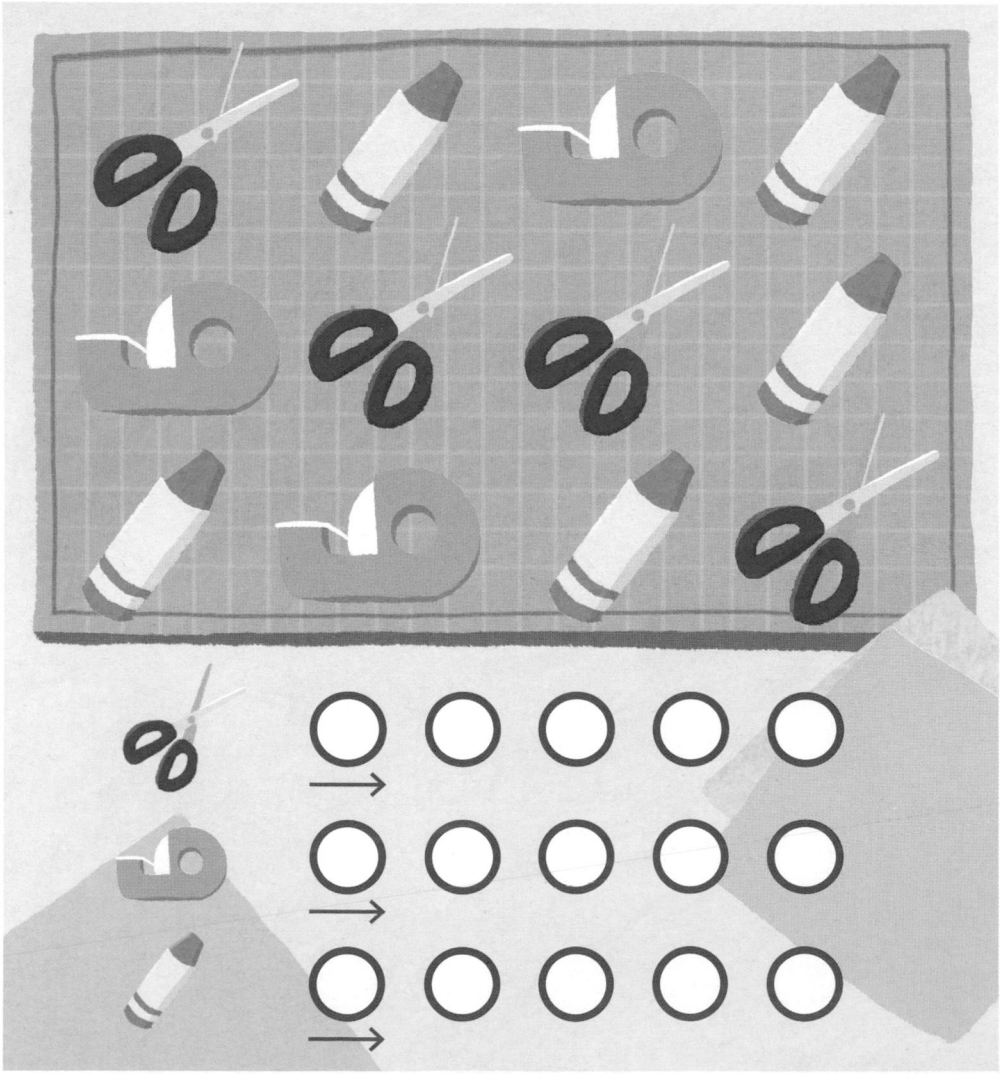

Level 2 ★★☆

Adventure Park Rides

Count the kids on each ride.
Then, put the matching number sticker on □.

To Parents Tell your child that the kids are grouped by rides, such as the airplanes and teacups.

Level 2 ★★☆

Which Is More?

Good job!

Follow the path from ➡ to ➡. Always go in the direction of the larger number of flowers.

To Parents Count the number of white flowers with your child at each junction, asking your child which is more every time. Repeatedly asking which is more will help them learn the rule.

Level 2 ★★☆

Which Is More?

Put a star sticker next to the larger number of mice, cars, and cupcakes.

Level 2 ★★☆

Which Is More?

Good job!

Draw a line from ➡ to ➡. Always go in the direction of the larger number of flowers.

Level 2 ★★☆

Count the Balloons

Count the balloons in each bunch.
Then, put the matching number sticker in the box.

Numbers and Trains

Level 2 ★★☆

Good job!

Count the trains in each group.
Then, draw a line to the matching number.

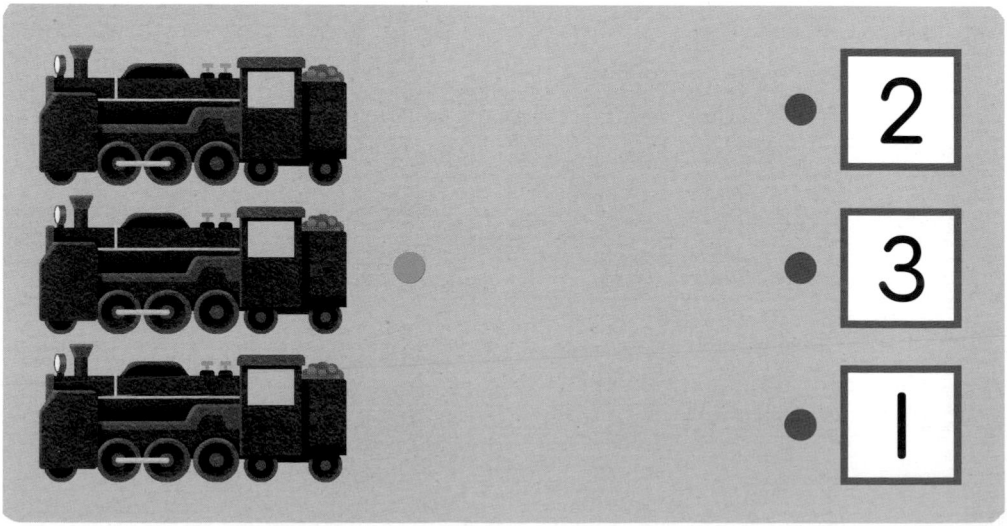

Level 2 ★★☆

Which Is More?

Put a star sticker next to the larger number of birds, cars, and doughnuts.

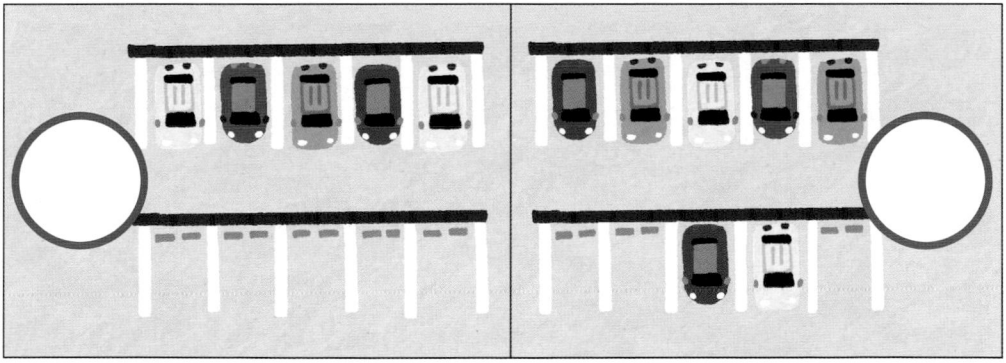

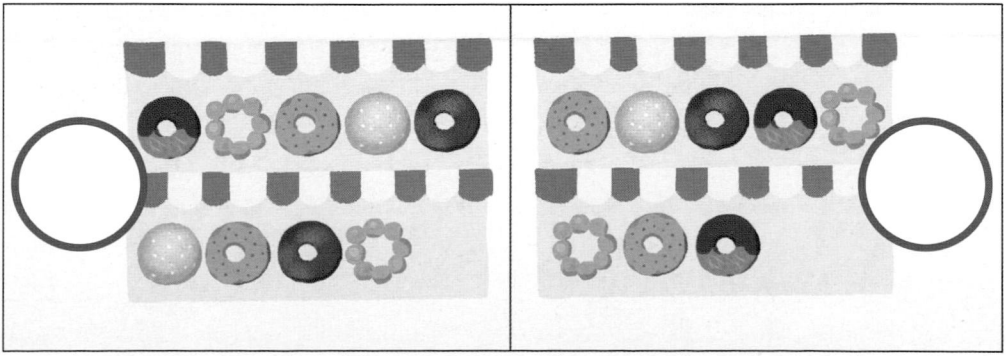

Level 1 ★☆☆

Color by Number

Color the number 3 in black.

Good job!

Level 1 ★☆☆

Number in Order

The numbers are in order from 1 to 3. Put number stickers in the blank spaces to fill in the train cars.

Level 1 ★☆☆

Color the Chicks

Good job!

Color the chicks with your favorite color.
Then, trace each number.

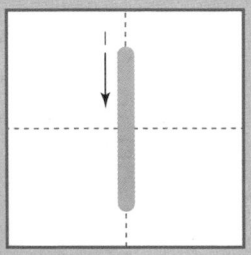

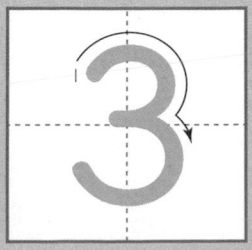

Level 2 ★★☆

Number in Order

Put number stickers in the blank spaces so they are in order from 1 to 10.

To Parents Before starting this activity, visit page 2 and count aloud from 1 to 10 with your child.

Level 3 ★★★

Match the Numbers

Draw a line from ● to ● to match the number of objects and stars. Then, draw a line from ● to ● to match the stars with the same number.

Good job!

four
4

three
3

one
1

five
5

two
2

Level 3 ★★★

Amusement Park Puzzle

Match the number on the sticker to the number in the gray box. Add the stickers to complete the fun scene.

Level 3 ★★★

Match the Numbers

Draw a line from ● to ● to match the number of objects and flowers. Then, draw a line from ● to ● to match the flowers with the same number.

Good job!

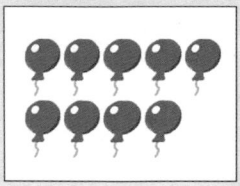

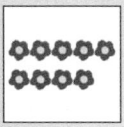

seven

7

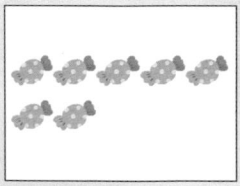

nine

9

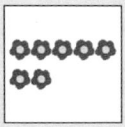

six

6

ten

10

eight

8

Level 3 ★★★

Halloween Night Puzzle

Match the number on the sticker to the number in the gray box. Add the stickers to complete the spooky scene.

Level 2 ★★☆

Which Is More?

Count the dogs, collars, and dog food. Which is more than the number of dogs—the collars or the dog food?

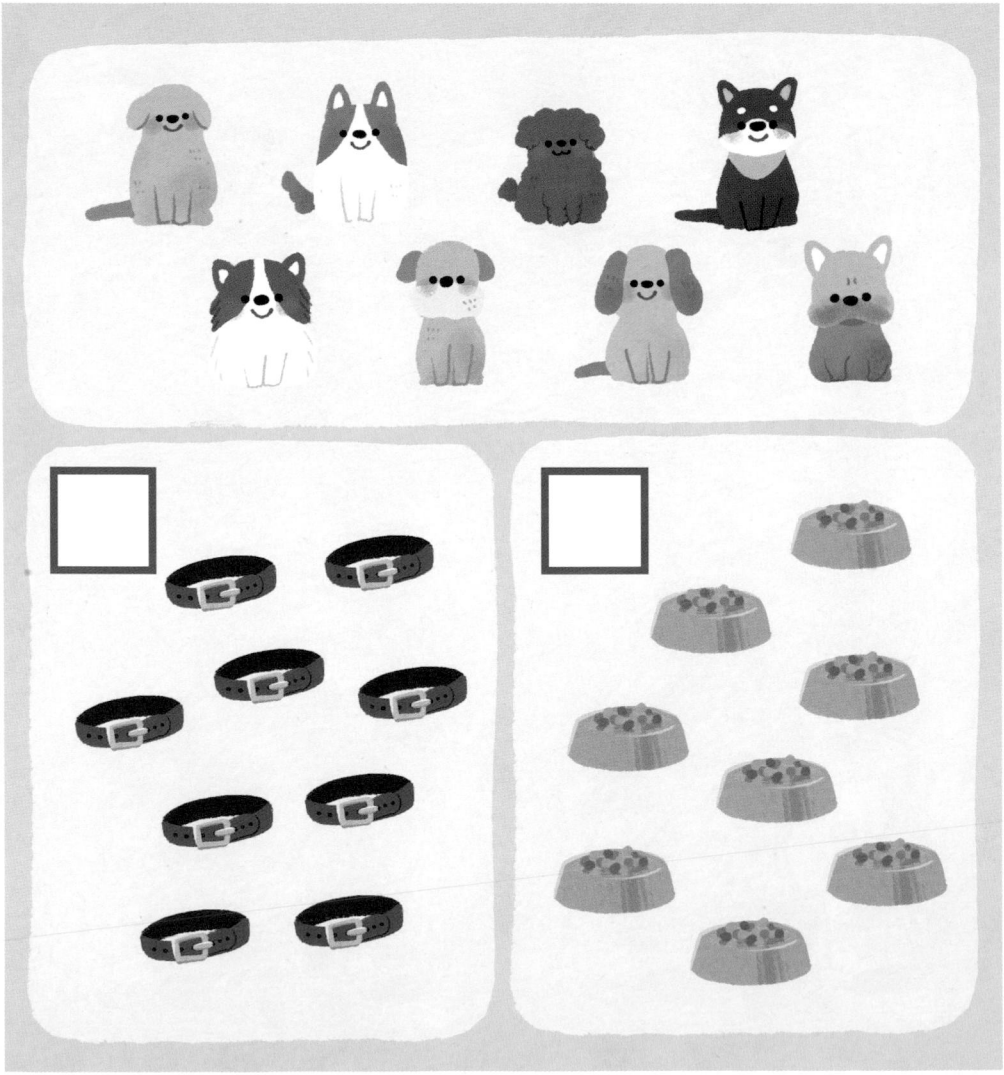

Level 2 ★★☆

Connect the Dots

Connect the dots in order from 1 to 10.

Good job!

To Parents Before starting this activity, visit page 2 and count aloud from 1 to 10 with your child.

Level 2 ★★☆

Which Is More?

Good job!

Follow the path from ➡ to ➡.
Always go in the direction of the larger number.

Level 1 ★☆☆

Trace the Numbers

Trace each number.

Good job!

Level 1 ★☆☆

Trace the Numbers

Good job!

Trace each number.